Seasons and You

AUTUMN

By Shalini Vallepur

KidHaven
PUBLISHING

Published in 2023 by **KidHaven Publishing, an Imprint of Greenhaven Publishing, LLC**
29 East 21st Street
New York, NY 10010

This edition is published by arrangement with Booklife Publishing

Edited by: John Wood

Designed by: Danielle Webster-Jones

Cataloging-in-Publication Data

Names: Vallepur, Shalini.
Title: Autumn / Shalini Vallepur.
Description: New York : KidHaven Publishing, 2023. | Series: Seasons and you | Includes glossary and index.
Identifiers: ISBN 9781534541290 (pbk.) | ISBN 9781534541313 (library bound) | ISBN 9781534541306 (6 pack) | ISBN 9781534541320 (ebook)
Subjects: LCSH: Autumn--Juvenile literature.
Classification: LCC QB637.7 V35 2023 | DDC 508.2--dc23

Manufactured in the United States of America

CPSIA compliance information: Batch #CSKH23: For further information contact Greenhaven Publishing LLC, New York, New York at 1-844-317-7404.

Please visit our website, www.greenhavenpublishing.com. For a free color catalog of all our high-quality books, call toll free 1-844-317-7404 or fax 1-844-317-7405.

Find us on

IMAGE CREDITS

All images are courtesy of Shutterstock.com, unless otherwise specified. With thanks to Getty Images, Thinkstock Photo and iStockphoto. Cover & throughout – By Africa Studio, Nataly Studio, By Charlotte Lake, y Tanya Sid, Bennian, Zheltyshev, lanych, PT1565, lewal1988, Tatiana Popova, oksana2010, Edward Westmacott, MARGRIT HIRSCH, Lizard. 4 – Nataliia Zhekova. 5 – Piotr Krzeslak. 6 – Sergey Novikov. 7 – kwanchai.c. 8 – Denis Kuvaev. 9 – Alexander Mak, Fotyma. 10 – Madlen. 11 – Alex Manthei. 12 – TDKvisuals. 13 –Lotus Images, Nattika, Bozena Fulawka, vitals, RomarioIen. 14 – Dennis W Donohue. 15 – Nynke van Holten. 16 – piya saisawatdikul. 17 – Boyan Dimitrov. 18 – StockImageFactory.com. 19 – Voraorn Ratanakorn. 20 – Nicky Rhodes. 21 – nelik. 22–23 – Honza Krej.

CONTENTS

Page 4 **Autumn!**

Page 6 **Autumn Weather**

Page 8 **Autumn Clothes**

Page 10 **Plants in Autumn**

Page 14 **Animals in Autumn**

Page 18 **Time to Celebrate!**

Page 22 **The End of Autumn**

Page 24 **Glossary and Index**

Words that look like this can be found in the glossary on page 24.

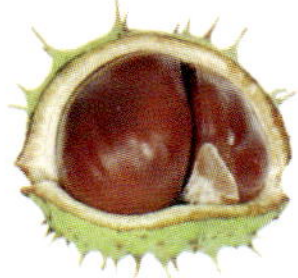

AUTUMN!

Autumn is a season. Most places in the world have four seasons. Each one has different weather.

Spring, summer, autumn, and winter are the four seasons.

Autumn is called fall in some countries.

Some places around the world do not have these seasons. Some places only have two seasons: rainy and dry.

AUTUMN WEATHER

The days and nights get a little colder in autumn. The leaves on some trees change color and fall off.

Do the trees in your area change color?

There can be a lot of rain and wind during autumn too. The days get shorter as the sun sets earlier.

AUTUMN CLOTHES

As it gets colder, you may need to wear a coat to stay warm. A hat and a pair of gloves will also help to keep you warm.

Rain boots keep your feet dry when it rains. Make sure you wear them if you go splashing in the puddles. Don't forget an umbrella too!

Do you like autumn weather?

PLANTS IN AUTUMN

In autumn, the leaves change color on some trees. They turn from green to red, orange, or yellow. The leaves fall off and cover the ground.

Have you ever walked on leaves on the ground? What did it sound like?

You may not see many flowers or plants during autumn. Flowers and plants do not grow well in cold weather.

The plants and flowers grow again when it is warmer in spring.

This tractor is harvesting corn.

Many different fruits and vegetables are harvested during autumn. They grow over spring and summer and are ready to be eaten in autumn.

Here are a few fruits, vegetables, and grains that are harvested during autumn.

Have you ever picked a fruit or vegetable before?

ANIMALS IN AUTUMN

During autumn, some animals may get ready for winter. Winter is too cold for some birds, so they fly to warmer places around the world.

Some animals gather lots of food during autumn. Squirrels gather lots of nuts and hide them. This means they have lots to eat in winter.

What animals live in your area?

Some animals eat lots and lots of food during autumn. This means they can hibernate or sleep through most of winter.

Some frogs hibernate during winter.

Bears usually sleep during winter. This means they spend autumn eating as much food as they can. They sleep in their den, which can be made in logs, caves, or trees.

TIME TO CELEBRATE!

There are lots of festivals around the world in autumn. Diwali is a Hindu festival of lights that comes from India.

People light fireworks during Diwali.

The Moon Festival is celebrated in China and other countries every autumn when there is a full moon. During the Moon Festival, people spend time with their families.

People eat moon cakes during the Moon Festival.

<u>Bonfire</u> Night is celebrated in the UK during autumn. People set off fireworks or go to see firework shows. They also build big bonfires.

Many countries around the world celebrate Halloween. People cut faces into pumpkins and dress up in costumes. They might watch scary movies and tell spooky stories too.

Do you celebrate any festivals during autumn?

THE END OF AUTUMN

Autumn happens at different times of the year around the world, but it is usually a season where it starts to get colder.

As autumn passes, the days keep getting shorter and it gets colder. It isn't long before winter arrives!

What's your favorite thing about autumn?

GLOSSARY

bonfire a large fire that is built to celebrate something

celebrated to have done something special for an important event

den an area where some animals live and rest

festivals special times of the year when people come together to remember or do something

gather to collect something

grains plants such as corn, rice, and wheat

harvested when fully grown crops have been picked

hibernate to sleep or rest during winter

Hindu having to do with Hinduism, one of the oldest religions in the world, which started in India

INDEX

animals 14–17
clothes 8–9
festivals 18–21
fruits 12–13
plants 6, 10–13, 17
trees 6, 10, 17
weather 4, 6–7, 9, 11